MW00355344

SCHOLASTIC

Scholastic Success With
Consonant Blends & Digraphs

by Robin Wolfe

New York • Toronto • London • Auckland • Sydney
Mexico City • New Delhi • Hong Kong • Buenos Aires

Teaching *Resources*

Scholastic Inc. grants teachers permission to photocopy the reproducible pages from this book for classroom use. No other part of this publication may be reproduced in whole or in part, or stored in a retrieval system, or transmitted in any form or by any means, electronic, mechanical, photocopying, recording, or otherwise without written permission of the publisher. For information regarding permission, write to Scholastic Inc., 557 Broadway, New York, NY 10012.

Cover art by Amy Vangsgard
Cover design by Maria Lilja
Interior illustrations by Sherry Neidigh
Interior design by Quack & Company

ISBN 0-439-55392-X

Copyright © 2004 Scholastic, Inc.
All rights reserved. Printed in the U.S.A.

1 2 3 4 5 6 7 8 9 10   40   09 08 07 06 05 04

Introduction

Reading is fun! Understanding phonics is a very important part of learning to read. Parents and teachers alike will find this book to be a valuable tool for teaching beginning readers. The basic skills addressed include recognizing two-letter and three-letter consonant blends and consonant digraphs. Children will enjoy playing word games and solving riddles as they complete the activity pages. Puzzles, word finds, and silly rhymes make learning fun. Take a look at the Table of Contents and you will feel rewarded providing such a valuable resource for your children. Remember to praise them for their efforts and successes!

Table of Contents

Scholastic Teaching Resources

What Is a Consonant Blend?

There are 26 letters in the alphabet. The vowels are **A, E, I, O,** and **U**. All the rest are consonants. Color each consonant yellow.

A B C D **E** F G H I
J K L M N **O** P Q
R S T **U** V W X Y Z

 *A **consonant blend** is when two consonants are side by side in a word, and you hear both sounds blended together. For example, you hear both the t and the r, blended together, in the word **tree**.*

Draw a red circle around the two consonants that are side by side.

tree   snow   fly   drum

 *Sometimes a consonant blend is made up of three letters side by side. The sound of each letter is blended together. For example, you hear the s, the p, and the r, blended together, in the word **spray**.*

Draw a blue circle around the three consonants that are side by side in the words below.

spray   screw   street

Blake the Bluebird

 Bl *makes the sound you hear at the beginning of the words* **Blake** *and* **bluebird.**

Draw a line from each **bl** word to its matching picture. Then draw a blue circle around the letters **bl** in each word.

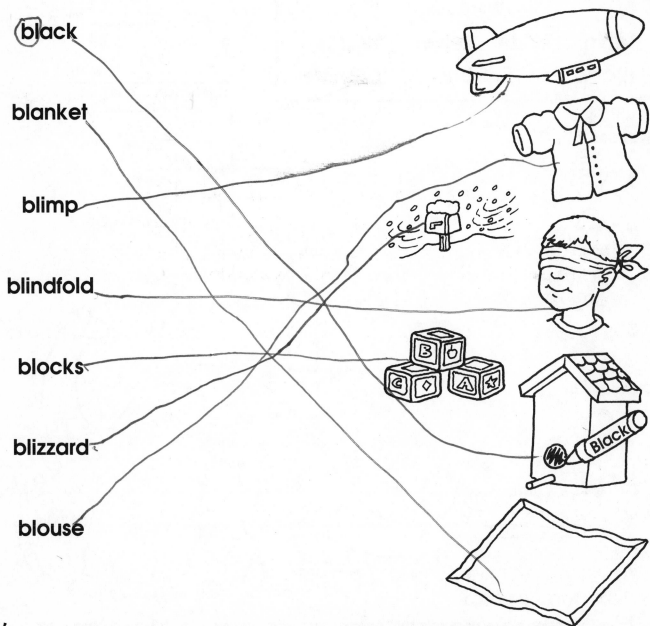

black

blanket

blimp

blindfold

blocks

blizzard

blouse

 You have this inside you. It is red. Your heart pumps it through your body. It begins with *bl.* **What is it? Find a picture of a heart. Draw it on another sheet of paper.**

Brady the Brontosaurus

 Br *makes the sound you hear at the beginning of the words* **Brady** *and* **brontosaurus**.

Brady the brontosaurus has made a puzzle for you. Use the picture clues and the Word Box to help you. Write the answers in the puzzle next to the correct number.

Word Box

brain   bride   broom   bridge

bread   brush   bricks   bracelet

Across

2.

4.

6.

8.

Down

1.

3.

5.

7.

 This makes a blue or purple spot on your skin when you get hurt. It is sore when you push on it. It begins with *br*. What is it? On another sheet of paper, write two or three sentences that tell about a time when you got hurt.

Clara the Clown

 Cl *makes the sound you hear at the beginning of the words* **Clara** *and* **clown.**

See Clara juggle the balls. Color the balls orange that have pictures beginning with **cl.** Color all the other balls blue.

Now write "Clara" on her costume.

 This is part of your room. You keep your clothes and shoes in it. It begins with *cl.*
What is it? On another sheet of paper, draw a picture of how yours looks right now.

Scholastic Teaching Resources

Crazy Crystal

 Cr *makes the sound you hear at the beginning of the words* **crazy** *and* **Crystal**.

Find out about the crazy things Crystal does in the sentences below. Fill in the blanks with **cr** to complete the words. Then write the number of the sentence in the box by the picture that matches it.

1. ___ystal wears a ___ash helmet to bed.

2. She makes ___ ispy, ___unchy ice ___eam.

3. She buys ___owns with her ___edit card.

4. She keeps her pet ___ab in a ___ib.

5. She feeds ___ackers to ___ocodiles.

6. Her glasses are ___ooked.

Dragon's Dream

 Dr *makes the sound you hear at the beginning of the words* **dragon** *and* **dream**.

This drowsy dragon wants to dream only about things that begin with **dr**. Color the pictures that it should dream about. If the picture does not begin with **dr**, mark an *X* on it.

Flora's Flowers

 Fl *makes the sound you hear at the beginning of the words* **Flora** *and* **flower**.

Flora loves to plant flowers. Her favorite ones are yellow flowers. Color the pictures that begin with **fl** yellow. Color all the other pictures orange.

 This word can mean what a boat does on the water. Or, it can mean a soda pop with scoops of ice cream in it. Or, it can be something big moving down the street during a parade. It begins with *fl*. What is it? Draw and color one of the meanings of this word on another sheet of paper.

Scholastic Teaching Resources

Freddy's Friend

Fr *makes the sound you hear at the beginning of* **Freddy** *and* **friend**.

This is a picture of Freddy's friend. Her name is Fran. There are nine things in this picture that begin with **fr**. Draw a red circle around each one.

fruit	frame	French fries	fringe
frog	**frown**	**freezer**	**freckles**	**frosting**

 This word names a day of the week. It comes after Thursday. It begins with *Fr*. **Which day is it? Tell what you like to do on that day.**

Scholastic Teaching Resources

Glen and Gloria

 Gl *makes the sound you hear at the beginning of the words* **Glen** *and* **Gloria.**

Glen and Gloria want to ask you some questions. Read each question below. Then find the answer in the Word Box and write it on the blank.

What is another word for happy?	**What kind of airplane is this?**	**How can I make my picture sparkle?**	**I cannot see the board. What do I need?**

How can I find out where Africa is?	**How will I keep my hands warm?**	**What will make my lips shine?**	**How can I fix this?**

Word Box

 glasses   glider   glue    globe

 lip gloss   glad   gloves   glitter

Grandma and Grandpa

 Gr *makes the sound you hear at the beginning of the words* **Grandma** *and* **Grandpa**.

Grandma and Grandpa are playing a card game. Whoever has the most cards with pictures of **gr** words on them wins. To find the winner, color each **gr** card green. Do not color the other cards.

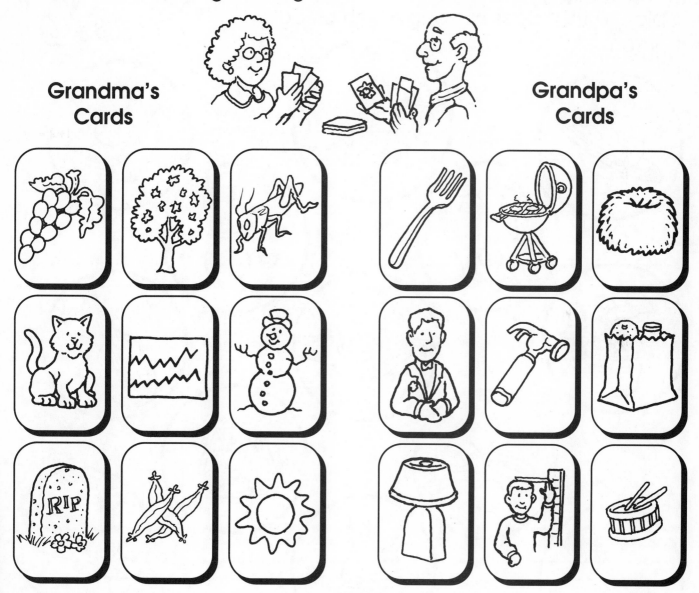

Grandma's Cards

Grandpa's Cards

Who won the game? Write your answer. _____

 For a woman to be a grandmother, she has to have some of these. She has pictures of them in her purse. They are her little sweeties. They begin with *gr*. **What are they? On another sheet of paper, draw a picture of your grandmother. Tell something nice about her.**

Mrs. Plum's Plates

 Pl *makes the sound you hear at the beginning of the words* **plum** *and* **plates**.

Mrs. Plum collects plates. Her favorite plates have pictures that begin with **pl**. Color the plates with **pl** pictures yellow. If a plate has a picture that does not begin with **pl**, color it green.

 It is good manners to use this word when you ask for something. It begins with *pl*. What word is it? Tell two other words that show good manners.

Name _____

The Prince's Problem

 Pr *makes the sound you hear at the beginning of the words* **prince** *and* **problem**.

Fill in the blanks below with the letters **pr**. Then read the rebus story. Color the pictures.

_ _ince   _ _oblem   _ _airie dog

_ _ofessor   _ _incess   _ _esident

_ _etzels   _ _etty   _ _esents

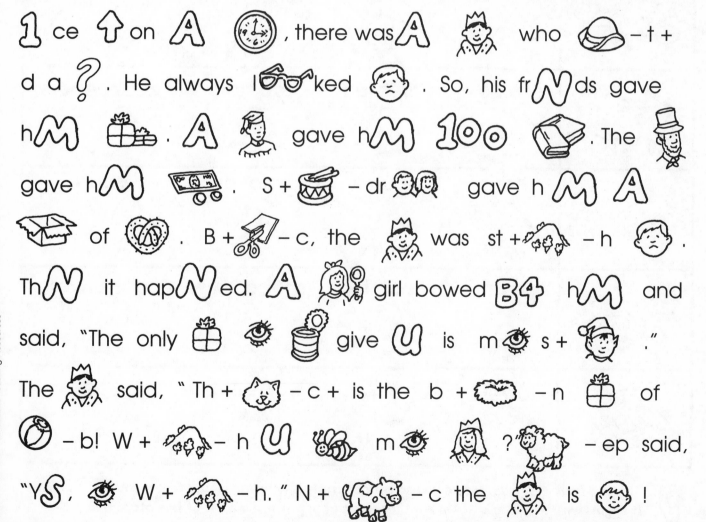

1 ce ⬆ on A 🕐 , there was A 👑 who 🎩 – t + d a ? . He always l👓ked 🙁 . So, his fr N ds gave h M 🎁 . A 🎓 gave h M 100 📚 . The 🎩 gave h M 💵 . S + 🥁 – dr 👫 gave h M A 📦 of 🥨 . B + ✂ – c, the 👑 was st + 🌿 – h 🙁 .

Th N it hap N ed. A 👧 girl bowed B4 h M and said, "The only 🎁 👁 🥫 give U is m 👁 s + 🎅 ." The 👑 said, " Th + 🐱 – c + is the b + 🪺 – n 🎁 of ⚾ – b! W + 🌿 – h U 🐝 m 👁 👸 ?" 🐑 – ep said, "Y S , 👁 W + 🌿 – h. " N + 🐄 – c the 👑 is 🙂 !

Name _____

Mr. Scott's Scarecrow

 Sc *makes the sound you hear at the beginning of the words* **Scott** *and* **scarecrow.**

Help Mr. Scott's scarecrow find some pesky crows. Find the word in each row that matches the picture. Color the crow underneath it black.

	bike	scooter	skates	wagon
	ant	ladybug	bee	scorpion
	scouts	firemen	doctors	zookeepers
	hat	purse	gloves	scarf
	clown	painter	scuba diver	bus driver
	towel	sink	scale	soap

 This is a feeling. It might make you scream or cry. It is how you would feel if you saw a ghost! It begins with *sc.* **What is it? On another sheet of paper, make a list of five other things that make you have this feeling.**

16   Scholastic Success With Consonant Blends & Digraphs

Scholastic Teaching Resources

Skippy the Skunk

 Sk *makes the sound you hear at the beginning of the words* **Skippy** *and* **skunk**.

Skippy the skunk has lost something.
Help him find it. Say the name of each
word below. If it begins with **sk**, color
the picture blue. If the picture does not
begin with **sk**, leave it white.

Sleepy the Sloth

 Sl *makes the sound you hear at the beginning of the words* **sleepy** *and* **sloth**.

Sleepy the sloth is too slow to play this game. You can play it for him. Look at the letters in each box. What letter comes between them? Use the alphabet to help you. Write the missing letter in the box above its clue. Then draw a line to the picture that matches the word you made.

A B C D E F G H I J K L M N O P Q R S T U V W X Y Z

1. R-T | K-M | H-J | C-E | D-F

2. R-T | K-M | H-J | O-Q | O-Q | D-F | Q-S | R-T

3. R-T | K-M | D-F | D-F | O-Q

4. R-T | K-M | D-F | D-F | U-W | D-F

5. R-T | K-M | D-F | C-E

6. R-T | K-M | T-V | F-H

7. R-T | K-M | H-J | M-O | F-H | R-T | G-I | N-P | S-U

 This is a kind of party. A girl or boy invites lots of friends to spend the night. They eat snacks. They play games. They watch movies in their pajamas. It begins with *sl*. What kind of party is it? On another sheet of paper, make a list of five games that you would like to play at this kind of party.

Smiley Smith

Sm *makes the sound you hear at the beginning of the words* **Smiley** *and* **Smith**.

Help Smiley Smith find the correct answers. He is looking for one picture in each row that begins with **sm**. Draw a smiley face in each box whose picture begins with **sm**.

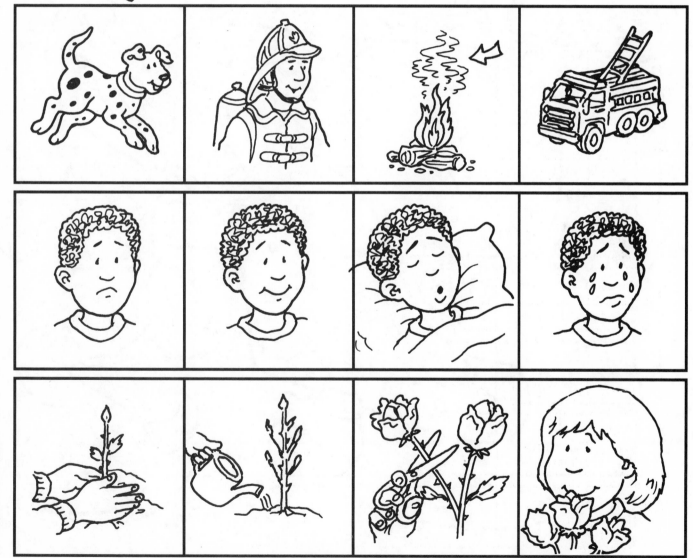

She knows all the answers on every test. She makes straight A's. She can learn quickly. What would you say she is? It is a word that begins with *sm*. On another sheet of paper, make a list of five things you would like to learn so you can be this word.

Scholastic Teaching Resources

Sniffles the Snake

 Sn *makes the sound you hear at the beginning of the words* **Sniffles** *and* **snake**.

Why is Sniffles the snake crying? He is lost! Help him find his way back to his mother. First, color only the pictures that begin with **sn**. Then use those clues to draw the path to Sniffles' mother.

 This is a snuffling sound some people make when they are asleep. It starts with *sn*. What is it? Pretend you are the voice for a cartoon bear who is sleeping all winter long. How would your bear sound?

Spike the Spider

Sp *makes the sound you hear at the beginning of the words* **Spike** *and* **spider**.

Spike the spider wants to catch **sp** words in his web. Color each picture that begins with **sp**. There are eight of them. Draw an *X* on the pictures that do not begin with **sp**.

 This begins with *sp*. **It is a green vegetable. It is good for you. Popeye eats it to make him strong. What is it? On another sheet of paper, draw a plate with this food on it, and some meat and bread to go with it.**

Switch-and-Swap

 Sw *makes the sound you hear at the beginning of the words* **switch** *and* **swap**.

Let's play a game called Switch-and-Swap. Look at the three-piece mini-puzzles below. They do not make sense the way they are. Cut them apart on the black lines. Switch the pieces around, swapping one piece for another, until the puzzle words match the picture. Glue them together correctly on another sheet of paper.

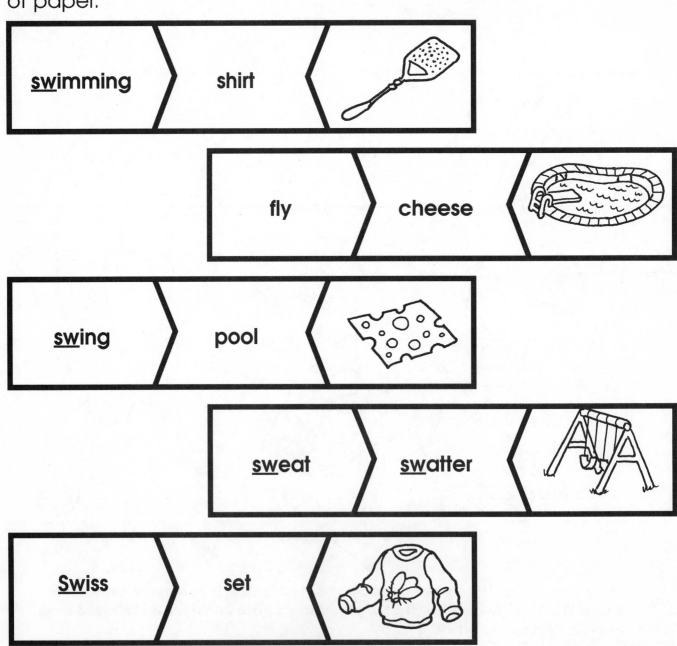

Stella's Stars

 St *makes the sound you hear at the beginning of the words* **Stella** *and* **stars.**

Stella has made up a game for you! Use the star code to make words that begin with **st**. Write the correct letter above each star. Then draw a line to match each word you made to the correct picture.

A   C   E   F   H   I   K   L   M   O   P   R   S   T   V

Twila's Twins

 Tw *makes the sound you hear at the beginning of the words* **Twila** *and* **twins**.

Twila's twins love to ask questions. Read each question below. Find a word that answers the question and write it in the correct bubble.

tweezers	Tweet! Tweet!	twelve	Twirl!	twister	twenty

This is part of a children's song. It is about a little star. The second line is "How I wonder what you are." The word begins with *tw*. What is it? On another sheet of paper, draw a picture illustrating this song.

Tracy's Trip

 Tr *makes the sound you hear at the beginning of the words* **Tracy** *and* **trip**.

Tracy is going on a trip. Help Tracy find ways to travel. Color all the things that move that begin with **tr**. Write *NO* on the things that do not begin with **tr**.

 This is a shape. It is not a circle. It is not a square. It has three sides and three points. It begins with *tr*. What is it? You can make one by touching your pointer fingers to each other and your thumbs to each other. Keep your thumbs very straight. Do you see one?

Scrambled Eggs

 Sometimes three consonants are blended together. All three consonant sounds are heard.
Scr *makes the sound you hear at the beginning of the word* **scrambled**.

Do you like scrambled eggs? Look at the words in the egg carton. Fill in the blanks with **scr**. Then write the number of the word next to the picture that matches it.

1. _ _ _ _apbook

2. _ _ _ _oll

3. _ _ _ _atch

4. _ _ _ _ewdriver

5. _ _ _ _ub

6. _ _ _ _eam

7. _ _ _ _eech owl

8. _ _ _ _ibble

 This begins with *scr*. **It is the glass part of a computer. It is the part you look at. Sometimes it is called the monitor. What else do you call it?**

Spray and Splash

 Spr makes the sound you hear at the beginning of the word **spray**.
Spl makes the sound you hear at the beginning of the word **splash**.

Splash! These boys are spraying each other to cool off. Look at the pictures in the drops of water. Then read the words that have **spr** or **spl** in them. Draw a line to match the words to the correct pictures.

splatter

splinter

split

spring

sprinkler

sprouts

spread

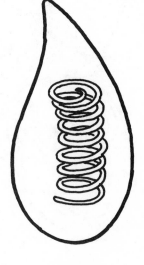

 They are teeny-tiny colored candies that go on top of cupcakes or cookies or ice cream. Yum! The word begins with *spr*. What are they? On another sheet of paper, make up a recipe for sugar cookies and include these in the instructions.

"Strike One!"

 Str *makes the sound you hear at the beginning of the word* **strike**.

Look at the pictures on the baseball caps below. If the picture begins with **str**, make red stripes on the cap. If the picture does not begin with **str**, color the whole cap yellow.

 This word describes some people's hair. It is the opposite of curly. It begins with *str*. **What is it? What kind of hair do you have? On another sheet of paper, draw and color a picture of yourself.**

Squeaky the Squirrel

 Squ *is a blend made up of two consonants,* s *and* q*, and the helper vowel,* u*. It sounds like* **skw***. It makes the sound you hear at the beginning of* **Squeaky** *and* **squirrel***.*

Squeaky the squirrel is looking for acorns. Look at the pictures in the acorns below. Find the word in the tree that matches each picture. Write it on the line.

Word Box

squid	squeegee
square	squeeze
squash	squad car

 What do you call it when you step in mud and it comes up between your toes? It begins with *squ.* **On another sheet of paper, draw a scene in which you are walking along and accidentally step in mud. Think about how your face will look when it happens.**

My Craft at Camp

 Some two-letter blends come at the end of a word.
The sound you hear at the end of **craft** *is* **ft.**
The sound you hear at the end of **camp** *is* **mp.**

Hi! I am having fun at camp. I am making picture frames out of sticks. Can you help me?

Draw a brown picture frame around each picture that ends with **ft.** Draw a red picture frame around each picture that ends with **mp.**

raft	**pump**	**stamp**	**stump**	**ramp**
jump	**soft**	**lamp**	**sift**	**hayloft**

 Some camels have one on their back. Some camels have two. It ends with *mp*. **What is it?**
On another sheet of paper, make up a funny story about a camel who had three of them.

Bring Kent a Drink

*The sound you hear at the end of **bring** is **ng**.*
*The sound you hear at the end of **Kent** is **nt**.*
*The sound you hear at the end of **drink** is **nk**.*

Look at each picture. Unscramble the letters to spell the word correctly. The words will end in **ng**, **nt**, and **nk**.

1. mtni _____

2. knub _____

3. tpian _____

4. grin _____

5. gfan _____

6. kksnu _____

7. npalt _____

8. nett _____

9. gristn _____

This means to shift or to bounce. This word is actually made up of two words that are hyphenated, both ending with *ng*. What is it? On another sheet of paper, draw you playing this game.

Scholastic Teaching Resources

Help Walt Milk

*The sound you hear at the end of **help** is **lp**.*
*The sound you hear at the end of **Walt** is **lt**.*
*The sound you hear at the end of **milk** is **lk**.*

It is time for Walt to milk the cows. You can help.
Cut out the pictures at the bottom of the page.
Glue them on the correct milk pail.

lp words

lt words

lk words

chalk	scalp	quilt	stalk	belt	walk
colt	salt	yolk	elk	bolt	gulp

A frying pan gets very hot. Someone puts an ice cube in the pan. Something will happen
to the ice. The word ends with *lt*. What will happen? Name four uses for ice.

The Pesky Wasp Nest

Sometimes two-letter blends come in the middle or at the end of a word.
The sound you hear in the middle of **pesky** *is* **sk**.
The sound you hear at the end of **wasp** *is* **sp**.
The sound you hear at the end of **nest** *is* **st**.

Help get rid of those pesky wasps nests. In each wasp nest below, fill in the blanks with **sk**, **sp**, or **st** to complete the words.

1. a ho__ __ital ma__ __

2. some cri__ __y toa__ __

3. the be__ __ ve__ __

4. a wri__ __ in a ca__ __

5. a roo__ __er on a fence po__ __

6. a__ __ing a que__ __ion

7. a ba__ __et for a si__ __er

8. a te__ __ on a de__ __

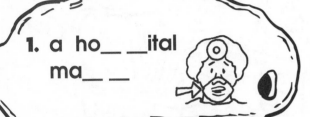

What Is a Consonant Digraph?

 When two consonants come together and make one new sound, these consonant letters are called **digraphs**.

Look at the man making new sounds in the digraph machine. He puts in two letters, but only one sound comes out!

Sh!

Now you try it! Look at the two letters. When the word comes out at the end, draw a green circle around the two letters that make the new sound. That is the digraph!

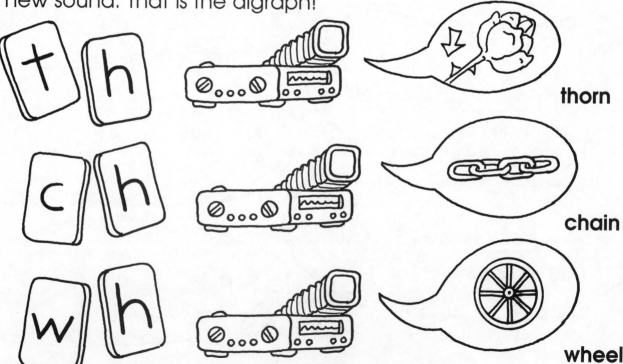

thorn

chain

wheel

Charlie the Chipmunk

 *When **c** and **h** come together, they make a new sound. You can make the sound by pretending to be a choo-choo train chugging up a hill. **Ch** makes the sound you hear at the beginning of the words **Charlie** and **chipmunk**.*

Charlie the chipmunk loves to play a game called "Which One Doesn't Belong?" Two pictures in each row begin with **ch**. One does not. Put a green *X* on the one that does not belong.

1.

2. 　　**3.**

4.  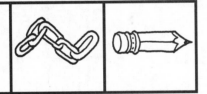　　**5.**

6.  　　**7.**

8. 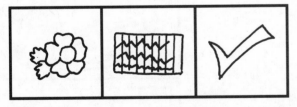 　　**9.**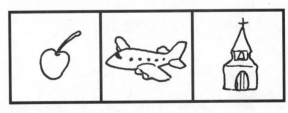

 It is brown and sweet. You make candy out of it. You might get some in a box on Valentine's Day. It starts with *ch*. What is it? Invent a new kind of candy no one has ever tasted. What crazy flavor will it be? Write an ad for it.

The Witch With an Itch

 *When the letters **tch** come together in the middle or at the end of a word, they make the same sound as **ch**. Tch makes the sound you hear at the end of the words **witch** and **itch**.*

Read each rhyme below. Fill in the blanks with **tch**. Write the number of the rhyme in the box beside the matching picture.

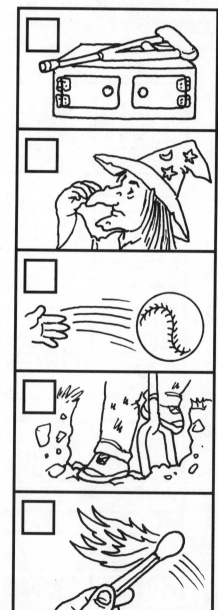

1. Once I saw a wi__ __ __

     Who had a rashy i__ __ __.

2. When I am digging di__ __ __es,

     The mud gets on my bri__ __ __es.

3. He makes the stick go "s-s-s-scra__ __ __,"

     And that's what lights the ma__ __ __!

4. Oh, I can't reach my cru__ __ __!

     I left it on the hu__ __ __!

5. The ball with small red sti__ __ __es

     Is used for throwing pi__ __ __es.

 This is how baby chicks are born. It is a word that means to break out of an egg. It ends with tch. What is the word? On another sheet of paper, draw a picture of a magic egg with something besides a chick coming out of it! Tell a story to go with your picture.

Sick Chick

 Ck *makes the* **k** *sound that you hear at the end of* **sick** *and* **chick.**

Poor little sick chick. He does
not feel like doing his
homework. Will you help him?
Fill in the blanks with **ck**. Then
draw a line to match each
word to the correct picture.

tru_ _

pi_ _ le

so_ _s

du_ _

clo_ _

ro_ _et

ni_ _el

bri_ _s

ne_ _lace

 This word has two *ck*'s **in it! It is something you carry to school. You put your books and
papers in it. It has pockets. What is it? On another sheet of paper, write a story about a
magic one and what it can do.**

Name _____

gh and ph
consonant digraphs

Laughing Elephant

 *Usually when **g** and **h** come together, both letters are silent, as in **fight**. But, sometimes **gh** can make the **f** sound, as in **laugh**.*

Write **gh** in each box to learn four new words.
Remember to make the letters **gh** sound like **f**
when you say them.

 rou ☐   cou ☐   tou ☐   enou ☐

 *When **p** and **h** come together in a word, they make the **f** sound, as in **elephant**.*

Read the funny poem below, or ask an adult to read it to you.
Draw a red circle around every word that has the letters **ph** in it.

Eletelephony
by Laura Elizabeth Richards

Once there was an *elephant,*
Who tried to use the *telephant*—
No! No! I mean an *elephone*
Who tried to use the *telephone*—
(Dear Me! I am not certain quite
That even now I've got it right).

Howe'er it was, he got his trunk
Entangled in the *telephunk;*
The more he tried to get it free,
The louder buzzed the *telephee*—
I fear I'd better drop the song
Of *elephop* and *telephong!*

 This is something you take with a camera. It is another word for snapshot or picture. It begins with *ph* and it ends with *ph*! What is it? Use a dictionary to find the word.

Scholastic Success With Consonant Blends & Digraphs

Shadow Shapes

 Sh *makes the sound you hear at the beginning of the word* **shadow** *or at the end of the word* **crush**. *This is the "Be Quiet!" sound.*

Look at the shadow shapes below. Fill in the blanks with **sh**.
It may come at the beginning, middle, or end of a word.

_ _ark   bru_ _   _ _oe   _ _eep   _ _ower

di_ _es   eyela_ _es   fi_ _ing   milk_ _ake

_ _ovel   _ _irt   spla_ _   _ _ell   _ _ield

Circle each word in the puzzle below. The words go down and across.

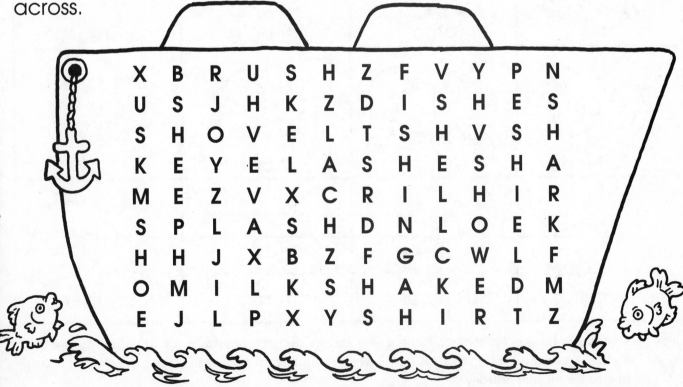

```
X B R U S H Z F V Y P N
U S J H K Z D I S H E S
S H O V E L T S H V S H
K E Y E L A S H E S H A
M E Z V X C R I L H I R
S P L A S H D N L O E K
H H J X B Z F G C W L F
O M I L K S H A K E D M
E J L P X Y S H I R T Z
```

That Thunder

 *There are two ways to make the **th** sound. When **t** and **h** come together, they can make the sound you hear at the beginning of **thunder**. Put your hand in front of your mouth and feel a little puff of wind when you say **thunder**. Sometimes, when **th** is in a word, there is no puff of wind. For example, put your hand in front of your mouth and say **that**. See, no wind!*

Draw a cloud around each word that makes a puff of wind when you say the th. Write *NO WIND* on top of each word that does not make a puff of wind when you say the th.

thumb	thirty	feather	moth
bath	father	thimble	one thousand
clothing	mother	thorn	math
breathing	leather	theater	brother

 This is a holiday in November. Families eat turkey then. It reminds us of the pilgrims and the Native Americans. It begins with *th*. What is it? On another sheet of paper, draw what you like to do on that holiday.

White Whales

 Wh *makes the sound you hear at the beginning of the words* **white** *and* **whales**. *To make this sound, blow out as you say the* **wh** *sound. Hint: Put your hand in front of your mouth to see if you are blowing out.*

Look at the whales swimming in the ocean. Color each whale white if it has a picture in it beginning with **wh**. Color each whale gray if it does not have a picture beginning with **wh**.

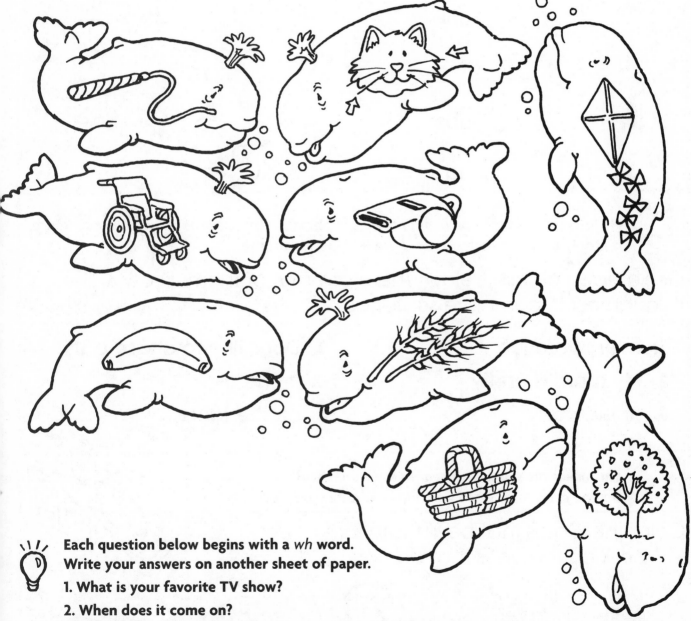

Each question below begins with a *wh* word.
Write your answers on another sheet of paper.

1. **What is your favorite TV show?**

2. **When does it come on?**

3. **Which do you like best: cartoons or game shows? Why?**

4. **Where do you like to watch TV?**

What About Us?

 Sometimes the digraphs **sh**, **ph**, *and* **th** *can be blended with* **r** *to make a new sound.* **Shr** *makes the sound you hear in the word* **shredder**. *That is a machine that cuts paper into tiny pieces.*

Write **shr** in the blanks to complete each word.
Then draw lines to match the words with the pictures.

_ _ _unk

_ _ _imp

_ _ _ubs

_ _ _ug

 Phr *makes the sound you hear in the word* **phrase**. *A phrase is not a complete sentence. It is only part of a sentence, so there is no period after it.*

Circle each phrase below. There are four of them. Draw a line through each complete sentence.

1. over the fence

2. Dogs like to chase cats.

3. My mom is pretty.

4. in the air

5. at the party

6. on the table

 Thr *makes the sound you hear in the word* **thrill**.
Do you get a thrill when you ride on a roller coaster?

Color the words that begin with **thr**.
Put an *X* on the ones that do not.

It's Your Turn to Shine!

Color only the picture that begins with the letters in the star.

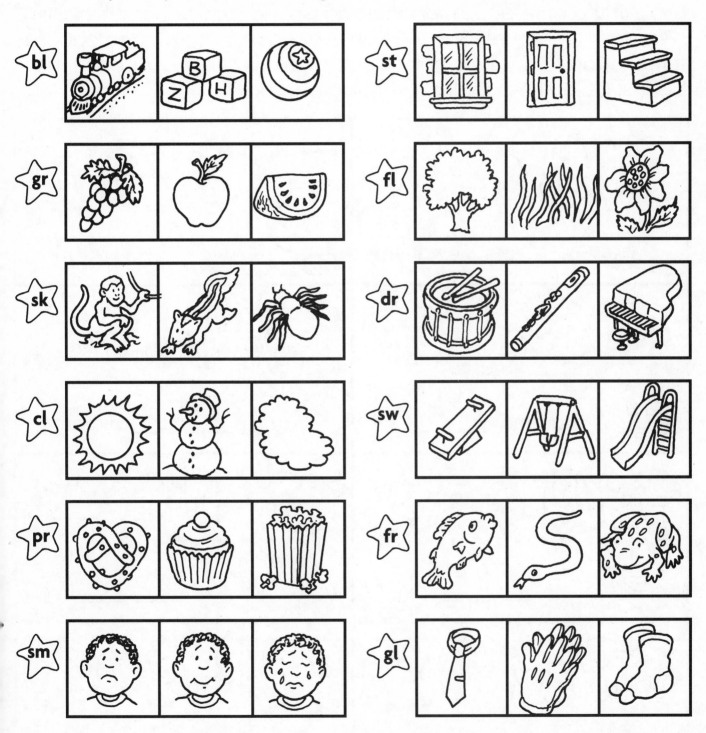

 This word begins with *bl*. It is what we call it when two consonants come together in a word and both sounds are spoken. Some of them are shown on this page. What are they called?

1-2-3, Please Choose Me!

 Three-letter blends include **scr, spl, spr, str,** *and* **squ.**

Look at the cute puppies in the dog pound. Each one is thinking, "Please choose me!" Say the name of each picture. Then choose three letters that will complete each word. Write the letters in the blanks. Color the puppies that were chosen.

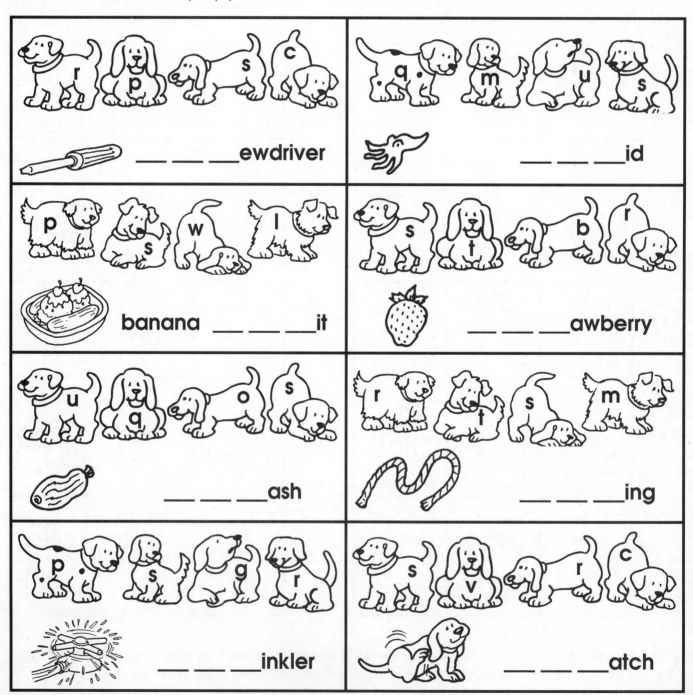

__ __ __ewdriver

__ __ __id

banana __ __ __it

__ __ __awberry

__ __ __ash

__ __ __ing

__ __ __inkler

__ __ __atch

Let's Match!

 Ending blends include **ft, mp, lk, lp, lt, nq, nt, nk, st, sp,** *and* **sk.**

Ladies and gentlemen, welcome to the game, "Let's Match!" Please look at the pictures in each box. Find two words that have the same ending blend. Color them. Mark an *X* on the one that does not match. Ready? Go!

 This is the sound a doorbell makes. It is two words. Both words end with the *ng* blend. What is the sound? If you could choose one famous person to ring your doorbell at your house, who would it be? On another sheet of paper, tell why.

Scholastic Success With Consonant Blends & Digraphs   45

Name _____

Digraph Dot-to-Dot

Write the correct digraph to complete the words in each box. Then connect the dots. Circle the word that is the same as the picture it makes.

ro_ _et

_ _eep

_ _umb

sh   ck   th

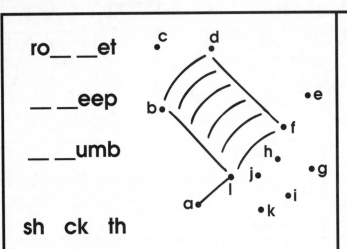

tru_ _

_ _ark

_ _ip

wh   ck   sh

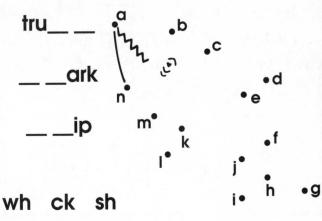

ba_ _

_ _air

tele_ _one

ch   th   ph

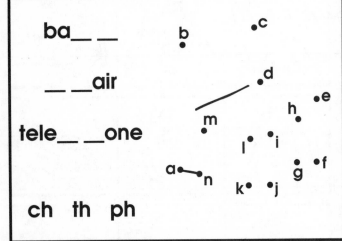

ele_ _ant

_ _eetah

fif_ _

ph   ch   th

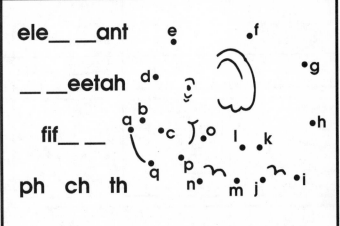

_ _ermos

cou_ _

_ _ort

gh   th   sh

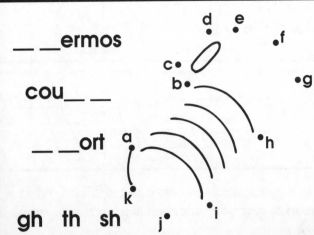

_ _erry

_ _eel

ca_ _

ch   sh   wh

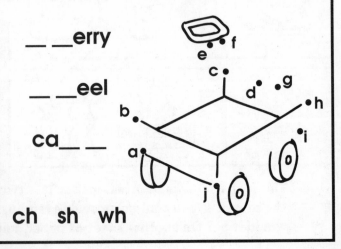

Page 4
Consonants: b, c, d, f, g, h, j, k, l, m, n, p, q, r, s, t, v, w, x, y, z; tree—tr, snow—sn, fly—fl, drum—dr; spray—spr, screw—scr, street—str

Page 5
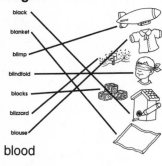

black
blanket
blimp
blindfold
blocks
blizzard
blouse

blood

Page 6
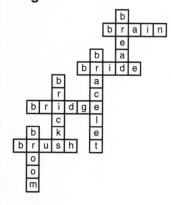

bruise

Page 7
cl words: clam, clap, clock, claws, climb, clothes, clouds, clover; closet

Page 8
1. Crystal, crash; 2. crispy, crunchy, cream; 3. crowns, credit; 4. crab, crib; 5. crackers, crocodiles; 6. crooked; 5, 1, 4, 6, 2, 3

Page 9
dr words: dress, drum, dragonfly, drain, dryer, drop, drill, drink, drive

Page 10
fl words: flag, flamingo, fly, flashlight, floor, flute, flipper, fleas, flowerpot or flower; float

Page 11

Friday

Page 12
glad, glider, glitter, glasses, globe, gloves, lip gloss, glue

Page 13
gr words: grapes, grasshopper, graph, grave, green beans; grill, groom, groceries, growing; Who won the game? Grandma; grandchildren

Page 14
pl words: planet, plow, plug, plant, place mat, playground, pliers, plus, plane; please

Page 15
Once upon a time, there was a prince who had a problem. He always looked sad. So his friends gave him presents. A professor gave him one hundred books. The president gave him money. Some children gave him a box of pretzels. But, the prince was still sad. Then it happened. A pretty girl bowed before him and said, "The only present I can give you is myself." The prince said, "That is the best present of all! Will you be my princess?" She said, "Yes, I will." Now the prince is happy!

Page 16
scooter, scorpion, scouts, scarf, scuba diver, scale; scared

Page 17
sk words: skate, skeleton, skillet, skis, skip, skateboard, skirt, skull, sky

Page 18
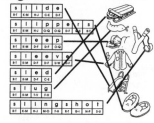

slumber party

Page 19
sm words: smoke, smile, smell; smart

Page 20
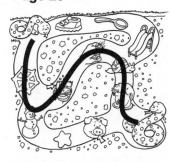

snowflake, snorkel, snap, snail, sneeze; snore

Page 21
sp words: sponge, spoon, spaghetti, spear, spur, space shuttle, spinner, spill; spinach

Page 22

swimming	pool
fly	swatter
swing	set
sweat	shirt
Swiss	cheese

Page 23
stamp, stool, steeple, stork, starfish, stapler, stick, stove

Page 24
1. Twirl!; 2. twelve; 3. twister; 4. tweezers; 5. Tweet! Tweet!; 6. twenty; twinkle

Page 25
tr words: tractor, train, tricycle, trolley, travel trailer (or just trailer), truck; triangle

Page 26
1. scrapbook; 2. scroll; 3. scratch; 4. screwdriver; 5. scrub; 6. scream; 7. screech owl; 8. scribble; 1, 8, 2, 6, 7, 4, 3, 5; screen

Page 27
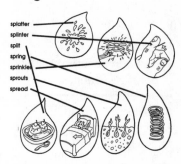

splatter
splinter
split
spring
sprinkle
sprouts
spread

sprinkles

Page 28
str words: string, street, stroller, straw, strawberries, streamers, strong, strap;
straight

Page 29
squid, square, squeeze, squeegee, squash, squad car;
squish

Page 30
ft words: raft, soft, hayloft, sift; mp words: jump, pump, stamp, lamp, ramp, stump;
hump

Page 31
1. mint; 2. bunk; 3. paint; 4. ring; 5. fang; 6. skunk; 7. plant; 8. tent; 9.string;
ping-pong

Page 32
lp words: scalp, gulp; lt words: quilt, belt, colt, salt, bolt; lk words: chalk, stalk, walk, yolk, elk;
melt

Page 33
1. a hospital mask;
2. some crispy toast; 3. the best vest; 4. a wrist in a cast; 5. a rooster on a fence post; 6. asking a question; 7. a basket for a sister; 8. a test on a desk

Page 34
(th)orn, (ch)ain, (wh)eel

Page 35
These don't belong: 1. fan;
2. pencil; 3. sleep;
4. paper; 5. nine;
6. flower; 7. airplane;
8. bicycle; 9. dinosaur;
chocolate

Page 36
1. witch, itch; 2. ditches, britches; 3. scratch, match; 4. crutch, hutch; 5. stitches, pitches;

hatch

Page 37
truck, pickle, socks, duck, clock, rocket, nickel, bricks, necklace;
backpack

Page 38
rough, cough, tough, enough;
words with ph:
Eletelephony, elephant, telephant, elephone, telephone, telephunk, telephee, elephop, telephong;
photograph

Page 39
shark, brush, shoe, sheep, shower, dishes, eyelashes, fishing, milkshake, shovel, shirt, splash, shell, shield;

```
X B R U S H Z F V Y P N
U S J H K Z D I S H E S
S H O V E L T S H Y S
K E Y E L A S H E S H
M E Z V X C R I L H A
S P L A S H D N L O R
H H J X B Z F G C W K
O M I L K S H A K E D M
E J L P X Y S H I R T Z
```

Page 40
Draw clouds around:
thumb, thirty, moth, bath, thimble, thousand, thorn, math, theater; Write NO WIND on: feather, mother, brother, clothing, father, breathing, leather;
Thanksgiving

Page 41
wh words: whip, whiskers, wheelchair, whistle, wheat

Page 42
shrunk, shrimp, shrubs, shrug;
phrases: 1, 4, 5, 6;
thr words: thread, three, throw

Page 43
bl: blocks; gr: grapes;
sk: skunk; cl: cloud;
pr: pretzel; sm: smile;

st: stairs; fl: flower;
dr: drum; sw: swing;
fr: frog; gl: gloves;
blends

Page 44
screwdriver, squid, banana split, strawberry, squash, string, sprinkler, scratch

Page 45
salt, belt; lamp, stump; chalk, milk; skunk, bunk; mask, tusk; king, ring; toast, nest; plant, paint; pump, stamp; string, song; ding dong

Page 46
1. rocket, sheep, thumb, picture—rocket; 2. truck, shark, whip, picture—shark; 3. bath, chair, telephone, picture—chair; 4. elephant, cheetah, fifth, picture—elephant; 5. thermos, cough, short, picture—thermos, 6. cherry, wheel, cash, picture—wheel